What People Are Saying About Steve's Reiki Books, DVDs, CDs

As always, Steve has written a Study Guide to take the powers we all possess and help us understand them and learn to use them. I believe this is why we are here, to learn all that we can do and be. Rather than fearing the unknown we should realize that all power comes from the Creator and that we are all part of one Eternal Being. Steve Murray helps us see the Divine in ourselves. *K.H.*

This program has to be the most convenient and realistic way to get started in the Reiki healing practice. I have tried several other Reiki programs in the past and Steve Murray's Reiki Ultimate Guides are the very best I have found yet. You will not be disappointed. *D.W.*

Recently I was diagnosed with a health issue so I decided to be in control of my own health again and restarted practicing Reiki. I'm grateful for these programs and I am now a Reiki Master certified through his program. I have recommended Mr. Murray's programs to my friends who suffer from health problems or stress. *R. M.*

Steve's books are like GOLD, as they are actually more comprehensive than the materials provided by most Reiki Masters to their students. I am sure that many Reiki Masters must be upset with Steve, as he divulges information that most Reiki Masters believe to be secret, including all the symbols up to Master Level and the attunement processes. Most Reiki books do not include this information, and have been very disappointing to me. *S.W.*

What's awesome about the DVDs is that you can take the attunements over and over again. As someone who was attuned in person by a Reiki Master over a decade ago, I can attest to the DVD attunements as being every bit as effective as in person. *H.M.*

I have nothing but great things to say about Steve Murray's program. All of his books are well-written, to the point, and very informative. The in-person attunement and Steve Murray's DVD Attunement felt the same to me and I plan to do Reiki 2 and Master Reiki through Steve Murray. He also can send you a really beautiful certificate for each level you complete! *A.J.*

I own all of Steve's Reiki books and Reiki Attunement DVDs and have found the attunements to be powerful and effective and the companion books (Reiki the Ultimate Guide, Vols.1-4) to be comprehensive and well written. I commend him for making a powerful healing tool available to all. *M.L.*

What can I say about Steve Murray and his work? I have been a Reiki practitioner for over a decade and I can tell you, Steve's books and DVDs are among my most treasured possessions on my book case. I see his work benefiting both existing Reiki practitioners and those just looking to get started. *B.F.*

Steve's DVDs and books empower you on whatever level you are interested in learning. He is a true teacher. You can read it, see it, and feel the energy. Thank you so much, Steve, for all your insightful information and for sharing all your knowledge with everyone in an affordable way. This was a smart investment for me. I am truly grateful and much more knowledgeable. *M.S.*

I like Steve Murray's books and DVDs because they are written by a man who truly believes in Reiki and what Reiki can do for everyone. Steve's introduction is quite honest and I know of others who share this philosophy and dedication to making Reiki affordable to people. *Y.S.*

This book is one of the best I've read in my 10 years of non-stop study in the healing energy arts, especially Reiki. Steve's approach is open, honest, and straight to the point. *R.M.*

Animal Psychic Communication
Plus
Reiki Pet Healing

Steve Murray

First Printing

Body & Mind Productions, Inc.

Animal Psychic Communication
Plus Reiki Pet Healing

Published by
Body & Mind Productions
9429 Cedar Heights, Las Vegas, NV 89134
Website: www.healingreiki.com
Email: bodymindheal@aol.com

First Printing August 2009

Library of Congress Cataloging-in-Publication Data
Murray, Steve
Animal Psychic Communication Plus Reiki Pet Healing
/ Murray, Steve – 1st ed.
Library of Congress Control Number 2008912110
ISBN # 978-0-9820889-0-6
Includes bibliographical references and index.
1. Reiki 2. New Age 3. Pets
4. Psychic 5. Spiritual 6. Healing

Cover design: Star Studios & Edyta Sokolowska
Photos: Edyta Sokolowska
Type design, production: Edyta Sokolowska
Editors: Sonya Baity, Carol von Raesfeld

Printed in the U.S.A.

DVDs-CDs-BOOKS

BOOKS BY STEVE MURRAY

Cancer Guided Imagery Program
For Radiation, Chemotherapy, Surgery,
And Recovery

Reiki The Ultimate Guide
Learn Sacred Symbols and Attunements
Plus Reiki Secrets You Should Know

Reiki The Ultimate Guide Vol. 3
Learn New Reiki Aura
Attunements Heal Mental &
Emotional Issues

Reiki The Ultimate Guide Vol. 4
Past Lives and Soul Retrieval
Remove Psychic Debris and Heal
your life

Animal Psychic Communication
Plus Reiki Pet Healing

Reiki The Ultimate Guide Vol. 2
Learn Reiki Healing with Chakras
plus New Reiki Attunements
for All Levels

Reiki False Beliefs Exposed
For All Misinformation
Kept Secret By a Few Revealed

Reiki The Ultimate Guide Vol. 5
Learn New Psychic Attunements to
Expand Psychic Abilities & Healing

DVDS BY STEVE MURRAY

Reiki Master Attunement
Become A Reiki Master

Reiki 2nd Level Attunement
Learn and Use the Reiki Sacred
Symbols

A Reiki 1st
Aura and Chakra
Attunement Performed

A Reiki Prosperity Attunement

Successfully Preparing for Cancer
Radiation
Guided Imagery and Subliminal
Program

Preparing Mentally & Emotionally
For Cancer Surgery
A Guided Imagery Program

Preparing Mentally & Emotionally
For Cancer Radiation
A Guided Imagery Program

Reiki 1st Level Attunement
Give Healing Energy To Yourself
and Others

Reiki PsychicAttunement
Open and Expand Your Psychic
Abilities

Reiki Healing Attunement
Heal Emotional-Mental-Physical-
Spiritual Issues

Reiki Psychic Attunement Vol. 2
New Attunements to Expand
Psychic Abilities

Preparing Mentally & Emotionally
For Cancer Chemotherapy
A Guided Imagery Program

Preparing Mentally & Emotionally
For Cancer Recovery
A Guided Imagery Program

Pain Relief Subliminal Program
Let Your Unconscious Mind Do It

5

Destroying Cancer Cells
Guided Imagery and Subliminal Program

30-Day Subliminal Weight Loss
Program Let Your Unconscious
Mind Do The Work!

Cancer Fear and Stress Relief Program

Successfully Preparing for Cancer
Chemotherapy
Guided Imagery and Subliminal
Program

MUSIC CDs BY STEVE MURRAY

Reiki Healing Music
Attunement Volume I

Reiki Healing Music
Attunement Volume II

Reiki Psychic Music
Attunement Volume I

Reiki Psychic Music
Attunement Volume II

Reiki Aura Music Attunement

Reiki Chakra Music Attunement

DVDs BY BODY & MIND PRODUCTIONS

Learning To Read The Tarot
Intuitively

Learning To Read The Symbolism
Of The Tarot

Mind Fitness Workout:
"Program the Mind for Weight
Loss as you Exercise" Dance Workout

How to Contact Spirits, Angels &
Departed Loved Ones:
A step-by-step Guide

Mind Fitness Workout:
"Program the Mind for Weight
Loss as you Exercise" Walking Workout

How to Contact Spirits Vol. 2
Learn to use a Spirit/Ouija Board
and Hold a Séance

Mind Fitness Workout:
"Program the Mind for Weight
Loss as you Exercise" Fitness Workout

Remove Psychic Debris & Heal Vol.1
Access a Past life

Remove Psychic Debris & Heal Vol.2
Soul Retrieval

Remove Psychic Debris & Heal Vol.3
Detach Negative Psychic Cords

Disclaimer

The Reiki pet healing methods in this book are not to be used in place of veterinary medical treatment. The methods are only meant to be used in conjunction with traditional veterinary medicine. When your animal is sick, always take the animal to a licensed veterinarian.

This book is dedicated to

All the vertebrates on the planet

Steve's Reiki Mission Statement

To make Reiki knowledge, guidance and Attunements available to everyone that seeks them. To make Reiki 1st, 2nd and Master Level Attunements affordable for everyone, so healing can be spread throughout the world.

Steve Murray

CONTENTS

The greatness of a nation and its moral progress can be judged by the way its animals are treated.

- Mahatma Gandhi

Introduction

Throughout the years my students have repeatedly asked me to write a book on Reiki pet healing, but with my other Reiki projects always stacked up, it was never possible. Because the emails kept streaming in, I decided I needed to make the time to write a book on that subject, so here we are.

My Reiki books and DVDs are written and produced primarily for my students. In all of these books and DVDs there are inevitably teachings that seem to cause some raised eyebrows among those in the "old school" healing community. This book is no exception. If you are from this community, just keep an open mind and use the information that resonates with you. In fact, that's the same advice I give all my students when reading my books and watching my DVDs. All rivers lead to the ocean, and my teachings are just one of the rivers that can take you there.

Books have been published on pet healing, some with Reiki and some without Reiki. The books on healing pets without Reiki identify the healing energy using numerous descriptions, such as, spiritual energy, love energy, heart energy, healing light, etc. As I have explained in my previous books, I believe there is only one Universal Life Force and this is the healing energy all healers have and use, and every person is connected to it. Other names for this Universal Life Force include Reiki[1], Chi, Mana, Holy Spirit, and the list goes on because every culture throughout history has had a name for it. So, in reality, both genres of pet healing books use the same Healing Energy, but show different methods on how to use it.

Unfortunately, in both genres of pet healing books, the methods of healing are sometimes complicated and the books either only briefly touch upon how to communicate with pets or do not mention it at all. With pets, I feel it is prudent if you are going to use Reiki (or whatever you choose to call the Universal Life Force), that you have an option to communicate with them before any healing is

[1] Of course, Reiki is what I choose to call it.

14

performed. With this in mind, this book is about teaching you an easy-to-learn Reiki pet healing method that includes a technique to psychically communicate with animals.

This book has three segments. The first defines the Chakras and the Aura, the second explains psychic communication with animals and shows you a method to accomplish this, and the third segment shows you my Reiki pet healing method step-by-step. The knowledge you acquire in the first two segments of the book will be used in the pet healing steps.

**I care not for a man's religion whose
dog and cat are not the better for it.**

- Abraham Lincoln

Animal Chakras
and Aura

God made all the creatures and gave them our love and our fear, to give sign, we and they are His children, one family here.

\- Robert Browning

Chakras

2

A Chakra[2] is an energy vortex within a psychical body that regulates energy (Life Force) into and throughout the physical body. Every animal has seven major Chakras and all seven Chakras work in conjunction with each other. In addition to regulating energy, each Chakra is responsible

---

[2] Chakra is a Sanskrit word meaning "spinning wheel" or "vortex."

for maintaining the health of specific organs, body parts (e.g., legs, arms, paws), glands, and nerves in its Area of Influence[3]. The Chakra's Area of Influence is determined by its location and surrounding area. In addition, certain major Chakras are responsible for maintaining the health of the physical body's internal systems. A few examples of the internal systems are the Reproductive System, Endocrine System, Nervous System, Urinary Tract System, Digestive System, Cardiovascular System, and Respiratory System.

Chakra Description

People who can see Chakras describe them as spinning wheels (Illus. 1) just beneath the surface of the skin that are connected to a vortex that generally extends a few inches from the animal's body. The vortex when viewed from the side looks like a compressed tornado. Chakras vary in depth and size depending on their location in the body and the dimensions and size of the animal.

Chakras spin clockwise[4] with the spin vibrating at different frequencies depending on which Chakra it is. The lowest rate of spin and frequency is the 1st Chakra with the spin and frequency increasing in each subsequent Chakra (the fastest or highest frequency being the 7th Chakra). The spin and frequency are also determined by the health of the Chakra. A blocked[5] Chakra's spin could be counterclockwise and the frequency would be lower than normal.

---

[3] More information on each Chakra's Area of Influence will be in the Reiki pet healing segment of the book.
[4] Clockwise when you are in front of the Chakra looking directly at it.
[5] "Blocked" is defined at the end of the chapter.

(Illus. 1) Chakra

Minor Chakras

There are many Minor Chakras (also called Secondary Chakras) throughout the body. Although you will not be working directly with the Minor Chakras, you should be aware that they exist. The Major Chakras are portals to Minor Chakras. The Minor Chakras assist the Major Chakras with their functions. The Minor Chakras are much smaller and vary in size, and are attached to joints, glands, the palms[6], feet, and nerve clusters throughout the body. People who can see Minor Chakras say they appear as spikes of energy emanating from the body rather than spinning wheels like the Major Chakras.

Chakra Block

Besides sending energy throughout the body, each Major Chakra is constantly exchanging information regarding the physical health of its Area of Influence to the other six Chakras. This exchange of information affects the entire body physically because Chakras make adjustments to their functions according to the information received from other Chakras. The energy and information travels between the major Chakras via pathways[7] called *Meridians*[8] or *Nadis*[9]. A Chakra can become "blocked" and this can slow down or prevent energy and information from flowing along these pathways. A "block" is a general term used to describe a Chakra not functioning well. A Chakra

[6] Reiki Healers use the Minor Chakras in the palms of their hands to channel Reiki.
[7] Since the Major Chakras are portals to the Minor Chakras, these pathways are connected to all Chakras, Major and Minor.
[8] What the pathways are called in Chinese energy healing.
[9] What the pathways are called in Indian energy healing.

becomes blocked when an illness or disease manifests in its Area of Influence or in the body system it maintains. A block in a Chakra prevents energy from flowing into and through it unimpeded. A "balanced" Chakra is a healthy Chakra with energy flowing into and through it easily and unhindered. In the Reiki pet healing segment you will learn how to unblock a Chakra so it can become balanced.

The dog represents all that is best in man.

- Etienne Charlet

Chakra Locations

3

Two of the seven Major Chakras are located at the top of the head in all animals. The remaining five Major Chakras each have a location on the back of an animal and each one of the five Chakras has a parallel location from this back location on the animal's front side.

The head is easy to recognize on vertebrates[10] making it uncomplicated to locate the two Major Chakras located there. With vertebrates, the five remaining Major Chakras are usually easy to find because the back locations are always along the spine with the front Chakras located directly opposite the back Chakras on the front side. Invertebrates[11] do not have a spine and their body shapes, including their heads, are very different, which makes locating their Chakras a challenge. If you find yourself working with an invertebrate, you will have to estimate the locations of the Chakras based on their body structure. There are several invertebrate illustrations with Chakra locations in the Chakra illustrations segment[12] to help give you a reference in locating Chakras on invertebrates. But, most likely you will be psychically communicating with and healing vertebrates, so the subsequent Chakra illustrations and location descriptions are for vertebrates.

Seven Major Chakras

Here are the locations of the seven Major Chakras starting from the base of the animal to the top of the head. Look at Illus. 2 to get an idea of the locations of the Chakras on the back of an animal and Illus. 3 for the locations of the Chakras from the front.

---

[10] Animals with an internal skeleton made of bone have spines and are classified as vertebrates.

[11] Invertebrates are animals without spines and that's 97 percent of all animals. There are so many species of invertebrates that the lack of a spine is often the only thing they share. A few examples of invertebrates are: insects, jellyfish, squid and crabs.

[12] Chakra illustrations are at the end of the book.

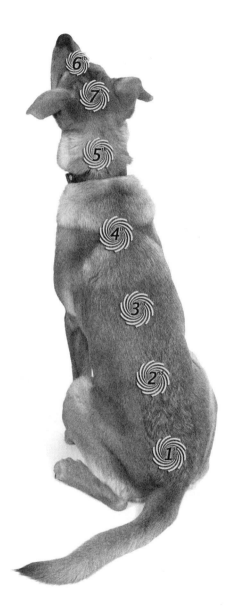

(Illus. 2) Chakras from the back

- The 1st Chakra, also known as the "Root Chakra" or "Base Chakra" can be accessed from the base of the animal in back of the body and the area directly opposite this location in the front of the body.

- The 2nd Chakra, also known as the "Sacral Chakra" can be accessed from the back of the body and the lower abdominal area in the front of the body.

- The 3rd Chakra, also known as the "Solar Plexus Chakra" can be accessed from the back of the body and middle abdominal area in the front of the body.

- The 4th Chakra, also known as the "Heart Chakra" can be accessed from the back of the body and the area where the heart is located in the front of the body.

- The 5th Chakra, also known as the "Throat Chakra" can be accessed from the back of the neck and the throat area in the front of the body.

- The 6th Chakra, also known as the "Brow Chakra" or "Third Eye Chakra" can be accessed in the area just above the center of the eyes.

- The 7th Chakra, also known as the "Crown Chakra" can be accessed at the top and in the center of the head.

The 6th Chakra is used exclusively in animal psychic communication. All seven Major Chakras are used in my method of Reiki pet healing.

(Illus. 3) Chakras from the front

Chakra Colors

Each Chakra emits a different light frequency as it spins, and this resonates as a color that can be detected by some people. If you cannot detect colors now, the more you work with the Chakras, eventually you may be able to see the colors associated with them. Seeing a Chakra's color can help with healing. For example, if the color is off, you will know that there might be a health problem in that Chakra's Area of Influence. The following are the most common colors associated with healthy Chakras:

- 1st Chakra – Red

- 2nd Chakra – Orange

- 3rd Chakra – Yellow

- 4th Chakra – The two colors most frequently associated with this Chakra are Green and Pink.

- 5th Chakra – Blue

- 6th Chakra – Indigo

- 7th Chakra – There are three colors most frequently associated with this Chakra: White, Violet, and Gold.

All of the animals except for man know that the principal business of life is to enjoy it.
- Samuel Butler

A Horse! A Horse! My kingdom for a horse!
- Shakespeare

Aura

4

All animals have a multi-layered energy field surrounding their physical bodies and it overlaps the extending vortex of each Major Chakra. In metaphysics, this energy field is called an Aura. Aura is a Latin word meaning "Light" or "Glow of Light." Scientists acknowledge that the Aura exists (although they don't call it an Aura). They define it as an energy field created by molecules, atoms, and cells in the body. As these elements interact, they create a subtle electrical and magnetic energy field that encompasses the exterior of the body. Of course, scientists either can't explain or they simply ignore the other aspects of the Aura that I will describe for you.

People who can see the Aura describe it as an egg or bubble shape of shimmering light and color combinations that radiate all around the physical body. (More on the colors of the Aura at the end of the chapter.)

The Aura is a composite of seven layers[13] with each layer extending out beyond the last. There are specific layers that reflect the physical, mental, emotional, and spiritual aspects of the animal. The Aura's development in each layer can be simple to complex, depending on the animal's evolution. Humans have the most complex Aura because of their development of language and communication skills, which in turn increases their Biological Intelligence[14] and emotional capacity. This also enables them to expand their spiritual awareness and search for spiritual fulfillment.

Seven Layers of the Aura

The first three layers of the Aura reflect the physical, emotional, and mental health of the animal. The outer three layers reflect the spiritual awareness and development of the animal. The fourth layer acts as a buffer and intermediary between the inner and outer three layers.

---

[13] These layers are also called auric layers, subtle bodies, energy fields or energy bodies.

[14] I define Biological Intelligence in Chapter 5.

The first layer is the Etheric Layer (Illus. 4). Ether refers to a state between energy and matter. This layer extends up to two inches away from the animal's body. Being the first layer closest to the body, it fits like a second skin and it is always in constant motion. This layer reflects a blueprint of the physical body. Physical signs of illness and injury can be detected in this layer by scanning[15], a process at which experienced Reiki Healers excel. Blockages in the Major Chakras can also be detected in this layer by scanning.

The second layer is the Emotional Layer (Illus. 5). It extends about two to four inches away from the physical body. This layer loosely resembles the animal's shape, but is not as defined as the Etheric Layer. Positive and negative emotions, including unresolved emotions, are reflected in this layer. The Emotional Layer is always in a state of flux because of the constantly changing circumstances in the animal's life that generate emotional reactions.

The third layer is the Mental Layer (Illus. 6). This layer extends about four to eight inches away from the physical body. This layer reflects the mental development and mental processes associated with the animal's biological intelligence. Mental health and/or mental issues are also reflected here.

The fourth layer is the Astral Layer (Illus. 7). It extends about eight to twelve inches away from the animal's body. This layer separates the three inner layers from the three outer layers. The Astral Layer is referred to as a bridge or

---

[15] When Healers pass their hand(s) over the physical body to detect health problems.

Etheric Layer

(Illus. 4) First layer of the Aura - Etheric Layer

Emotional Layer

(Illus. 5) Second layer of the Aura - Emotional Layer

Mental Layer

(Illus. 6) Third layer of the Aura - Mental Layer

Astral Layer

(Illus. 7) Fourth layer of the Aura - Astral Layer

portal between the physical world and the spiritual world, the physical world being the body and the first three Aura Layers and the spiritual world the next three layers outside of the Astral Layer.

The combined distance from the body of the first four layers of the Aura is usually a maximum of 12 inches with all animals. The outer three layers are where the distance from an animal's body can vary the most. This distance is predicated on the spiritual development and awareness of the animal. The last three layers of the Human Aura can extend from the body another four feet or so beyond the 12 inches of the first four layers. With highly spiritually evolved Humans, their Auras can extend outward perhaps seven feet or more.

The distance from the body of the last three layers of the Aura with non-human animals depends on their spiritual development, and it is difficult to give guidelines[16] on this. This is why in my description of the last three Aura Layers I give only the distance from a human body and no illustrations. But with Reiki pet healing, what is important is the knowledge of the distance of 12 inches from the animal's body of the Aura's first four layers.

The fifth layer is the Etheric Template Layer, and it extends about one to two feet away from the physical body in Humans. It keeps the first four layers of the Aura in place and it reflects the physical body spiritually.

---

[16] Although you might be able to see or sense how far the last three layers extend with some animals.

40

The sixth layer is the Celestial Layer. It extends about two to three feet away from the Human body. The Celestial Layer reflects unconditional love, spiritual ecstasy, and the spiritual emotions of the animal's soul.

The seventh layer is the Ketheric Layer and it extends about three to five feet away from a Human's body, depending on the level of spiritual awareness the person has developed. This layer reflects all the animal's spirituality and contains a template of all the information reflected in the other six Aura Layers. While the other Aura Layers dissipate after the physical death of the body, this layer continues to exist for eternity. This layer's information can be accessed in the Akashic Records[17].

Aura Blocks

The Aura can have energy blocks in the Emotional and Mental Layers that can actually slow down or prevent Animal Psychic Communication and pet healing. The blocks are created by unresolved emotional and mental problems the animal might have. I call the unresolved emotional and mental problems Psychic Debris[18].

---

[17] A dimension that stores all information on past lives. Edgar Cayce accessed the records to help his clients with health issues. My *Reiki Ultimate Guide Vol. 4* shows you how to access the Akashic Records.
[18] I write about releasing Psychic Debris in many of my books. I also have a DVD trilogy titled *Remove Psychic Debris & Heal*. More detailed information on Psychic Debris in Chapter 13.

Aura Colors

The energy of each layer of the Aura vibrates at a different frequency that produces color. The energy vibration can change, thereby producing different colors depending on the physical, mental, emotional, and spiritual conditions and/or circumstances being experienced by the animal. The majority of people cannot see the Aura or its colors, although experienced Reiki Healers can sense and feel its colors. Here are the most common colors of a healthy Aura reported by people who can see it.

- Etheric Layer: Shades of blue or gray.

- Emotional Layer: All the colors in the rainbow, with positive emotions creating bright colors and negative emotions creating dark colors.

- Mental Layer: A bright shade of yellow that becomes brighter during a mental process.

- Astral Layer: A brightly colored rosy hue.

- Etheric Template Layer: Dark blue or cobalt blue.

- Celestial Layer: Bright pastel colors.

- Ketheric Layer: Bright gold with tiny golden silver threads spreading throughout the layer.

The Aura, Chakras, and the physical body are a complete unit. This means you will be working within the Aura when you are psychically communicating with or healing an animal.

Animals are such agreeable friends - they ask no questions, they pass no criticisms.

- George Eliot

**A bird does not sing because it has an answer.
It sings because it has a song.**

- Chinese Proverb

ANIMAL PSYCHIC COMMUNICATION

Our task must be to free ourselves - by widening our circle of compassion to embrace all living creatures and the whole of nature and its beauty.

- Albert Einstein

Living Beings

5

All "Living Beings" are connected mentally, emotionally, and spiritually through time and space with the same Universal Life Force (Reiki, Chi, Mana, etc.) flowing through their physical bodies. All animals[19] are Living Beings and yes, Humans are animals. Let me back up here and give

---

[19] "Animal" is derived from the Latin word "Anima" or "Anim" which means having a spirit or soul.

the definition scientists give of animals, in case you have any doubt you are an animal. Animals are comprised of eukaryotes[20] and have a well-defined shape and can move voluntarily. Animals also actively acquire food and digest it internally and have sensory and nervous systems that allow them to respond rapidly to stimuli and sexual reproduction. Well, that definition includes dogs, cats, horses, birds, reptiles, etc., and us, the Human animal. Welcome to Animalia[21].

My main point of defining animals is that to successfully communicate psychically with other animals it is crucial you understand and accept that you are indeed an animal yourself. By doing so, this will eliminate any attitudes or beliefs you might have that you are a superior species and not connected to non-human animals. Having attitudes or beliefs like this, or similar ones, will slow down or even block and prevent any chance of psychic communication with all animals.

Biological Intelligence

The Human animal and each species of non-human animals possess their own unique Biological Intelligence that is used best in the environment in which they have evolved. I believe this intelligence in all animals has two things in common. One, it enables them to comprehend mental images and associate meaning to mental images. Two, it makes it possible for all animals to be capable of

---

[20] Eukaryote is a single-celled or multi-cellular organism whose cells contain a distinct membrane-bound nucleus.

[21] Animalia is defined as the realm of animals; the animal kingdom.

experiencing feelings (e.g., fear, stress, joy, love, pain). Biological Intelligence is the reason you can have psychic communication with all animals. Now this brings me to the definition of Psychic. "Psychic" is derived from a Greek word meaning "mind." Animal Psychic Communication is really Animal Mind Communication. In the next chapters you will learn how to communicate with animals through the mind.

Animals can communicate quite well. And they do. And generally speaking, they are ignored.

- Alice Walker

Psychic Abilities

6

Animal Psychic Communication consists of sending information or receiving information through Biological Intelligence. Sending is pretty straight-forward. It is conveying information you want the animal to understand and/or act upon. An example of this would be sending information to the animal to influence behavior during a training session.

Receiving information covers several scenarios. It can be receiving information from an animal's response to information sent, which can turn into a back and forth communication; or, it can be receiving information without first sending information. If you receive information first, that could also lead to a back and forth communication.

Four Psychic Abilities

There are four distinct psychic abilities that are used in sending and receiving information in Animal Psychic Communication. They are Clairsentience, Clairvoyance, Clairaudience, and Telepathy. All four abilities can transcend time and space. Let's take a look at each of the four Psychic abilities.

Clairsentience

Clairsentience is referred to as "clear feeling" or "clear knowing" and is associated with the 2nd Chakra. It is receiving information through feelings, bodily sensations, and sometimes smells. When your Clairsentience is developed, you can sense and know what you can't see and understand what you feel. Using this psychic ability you will sense and know the information received from an animal and be able to interpret the meaning.

Clairsentience is the most common psychic ability experienced by people with their own animals. A few examples of this: feeling and understanding an animal's sadness when leaving or joy upon returning; sensing an animal's dislike of a person who has entered the house.

Clairvoyance

Clairvoyance is the psychic ability referred to as "clear sight" or "clear seeing." It is associated with the 6th Chakra, which is sometimes called the "third eye" or the "mind's eye." It is the psychic ability of receiving information mentally through images. These images can be in black and white or in color.

We subconsciously convert thoughts and words into images and this helps to interpret Clairvoyance information received from animals. Most animals have a developed ability of Clairvoyance.

Clairaudience

Clairaudience is referred to as "clear hearing" or "having psychic ears" and is associated with the 5th Chakra. It is the psychic ability of receiving information through words and sounds. This psychic information can be heard from within or outside your physical body.

Telepathy

Information obtained by Clairsentience, Clairvoyance, and Clairaudience has to transcend time and space to be sent or received by an animal's Biological Intelligence. Telepathy is the process by which this is done, and it also refers to the ability to do this. Think of Telepathy as tapping into a wireless invisible phone line to send and receive psychic information like images, feelings, sounds, etc., animal to animal. This concept is easy to grasp if you compare Telepathy to the technology used to send wireless information from one computer's hard drive (Artificial Intelligence) to another computer's hard drive. Just like in Telepathy, this wireless exchange from computer to computer can include images, sounds, and feelings, but with computers, the feelings are represented in text messages.

I have been studying the traits and dispositions of the "lower animals" (so called) and contrasting them with the traits and dispositions of man. I find the result humiliating to me.

- Mark Twain

**An animal's eyes have the power
to speak a great language.**

- Martin Buber

Images, Not Language

7

There are Animal Psychic books that teach methods to psychically communicate with animals using Telepathy and the English language (or your own native language if not English). The books ultimately instruct you to ask the animal a question or questions in English through Telepathy.

After receiving the question(s), the books explain that the animal will be able to comprehend English and respond back in English by Telepathy. I find it difficult to wrap my conscious mind around the concept that animals can instantly understand and then know English to speak it mentally. The books give various reasons why this occurs, from the animal tapping into Universal Knowledge, to an invisible translator box making the language conversion possible. In fact, many people are not open to the concept that animals can instantly understand and (mentally) speak various languages, which makes it problematic, if not impossible for them to learn how to psychically communicate with animals. You have to believe in a teaching to use it effectively.

Imagine how difficult it would be if you were in a room with another person who understood and spoke only Chinese and needed to communicate with that person by Telepathy in English. It would be impossible for the person who spoke Chinese to understand you and for you to understand the person when he or she responded back telepathically. Unless the knowledge and the ability to understand and then speak each other's language transpired instantly, no communication would occur.

Now, if you and the Chinese-speaking person could send or receive mental images instead of language, there could be a basic understanding of what was being sent and received. The reason being, both of you would have a universal comprehension of what the mental images represent. That's the type of animal psychic communication

I teach, sending images, not words. And, it is achievable for most people. On the other hand, the majority of people are open to the concept of Telepathy taught in animal psychic books. This openness is possible because they have briefly experienced receiving psychic information through Telepathy in their own lives or know of someone who has. A few examples of this are: feeling a person's emotional pain, hearing the phone ring and se eing a mental image of the person calling, and knowing, seeing, or feeling loved ones in distress or in danger when they actually are. These brief, fleeting psychic experiences are possible because of inherent psychic abilities that every person has, but are now basically dormant.

Intrinsic Psychic Abilities

My belief is that all Humans have intrinsic psychic abilities that are now dormant because of lack of use. These psychic abilities evolved many thousands of years ago in Humans for purposes of communication and survival. The psychic abilities were used for up-close and personal communication because spoken language was non-existent to limited in early Humans. Psychic abilities also came into play for survival when information[22] needed by the tribe or family unit was communicated to them from a distance from one or more of the members. As Humans developed, so did their speaking skills, languages, and methods of communication over long distances. Psychic abilities were not needed, thus becoming dormant.

---

[22] Such as the whereabouts of food, location of enemies, weather conditions, where to meet or when arriving, etc.

Current examples of psychic abilities in Humans are the Aboriginal Australians[23]. For tens of thousands of years they lived in the remote areas of Australia and did not evolve like the rest of civilization. When they were finally discovered by modern civilization it was documented that they were still using psychic abilities up close and from a distance. To this day the native Australians are still known for their psychic ability to communicate over long distances.

The good news is you can learn to use your intrinsic psychic abilities in communicating with animals and I will show you how in the next chapters.

---

[23] Australia's indigenous people who migrated from Asia about 30,000 years ago.

I don't believe in the concept of hell, but if I did, I would think of it as filled with people who were cruel to animals.

- Gary Larson

I am in favor of animal rights as well as human rights. That is the way of a whole human being.

- Abraham Lincoln

Step-By-Step

8

Intent and visualization are very integral parts of Animal Psychic Communication. Intent is the state of mind when you are focused on a specific purpose, a course of action. Without intent, animal psychic communication would not be possible. Visualization is a process of mentally creating and depicting an image or images in your mind from your words and thoughts. Without visualization, Animal Psychic Communication would be extremely difficult.

The following are the steps in Animal Psychic Communication. You do not have to be in a quiet area to communicate with an animal. With these steps you will be able to communicate with an animal in their own environment (a house, outdoors, in a zoo, etc.), which most of the time will not be quiet. As an option, when you are first learning how to psychically communicate with animals, you can practice in a quiet area until you are skilled with the steps.

If you are only receiving information, you will leave out Step #5. Use the Chakra illustrations at the end of the book if you need help locating the 6th Chakra of any animal with which you will be psychically communicating.

The Steps

1. Connect

2. Chakra and Aura Clearing

3. Enter the Zone

4. Visualize

5. Send Information

6. Receive Information

7. Ending Communication

Now, I will explain each step.

Connect

It is important that you establish your intention to communicate with an animal as the first step (Illus. 8), whether it is to send information or receive information. You only need to do this once at the start of the communication process, even though you might end up sending and receiving information back and forth to the animal. Establishing the initial intent sets up the psychic connection needed between you and the animal to start the communication. Here's how you do it.

Once you are situated in an area with an animal you can see[24] and would like to communicate with, you need to determine what information you want to send to the animal and then state this to yourself silently with your own words. For example: "I am going to communicate with Sammy (a pet dog) and send him a message that I want him to start using his new dog door." Or, if you are going to communicate with an animal you don't have a name for, you would state the kind of animal and its location and the message (e.g., I am going to communicate with the bird in the backyard tree and ask it to start singing.)

If you are going to receive information first, not send a message, your intent is going to be stated differently. The wording will depend on what information you are trying to receive, generic or specific. An example of generic intent stated silently would be: "I am going to receive information

---

[24] If you cannot see the animal, you can do long distance psychic communication described at the end of the chapter.

Establish your intention to communicate with an animal as the first step, whether it is to send information or receive information.

Illus. 8

from Sammy." An example of specific intent stated silently would be: "I'm going to receive information from Sammy on why he barks at noon every day."

The same rule applies for the intent to receive information from an animal for which you don't have a name. You state the kind of animal and its location and what information you would like to receive. An example of generic intent stated silently in this scenario would be: "I am going to receive information from the bird in the back yard in the tree." An example of specific intent stated silently would be: "I am going to receive information from the bird in the backyard on why it isn't singing."

When using generic intent to receive information, you really don't know what type of information you will receive from the animal. And, what you receive may be a surprise, not what you were expecting.

Chakra and Aura Clearing

The next step is clearing your Aura's Mental and Emotional Layers and 6th Chakra of any possible blockages. Then you must clear the animal's 6th Chakra and its Aura's Mental and Emotional Layers of any blockages the animal might have. This clearing dissolves any blockages[25] that might be in the Aura or Chakra which would prevent or slow down the communication between the two of you.

---

[25] If there are any blockages in your Aura or 6th Chakra, the clearing might only temporarily dissolve the blockage(s). The Reiki Ultimate Guides Vol. 2 (Chakras) and Vol. 3 (Aura) address this issue of returning blockages.

There are two methods to perform the Clearing. In the first method, you visualize a white or golden sphere of light the size of your forehead about 12 inches[26] in front of your 6th Chakra (Illus. 9) for a few seconds, then visualize the sphere going through the Aura into your Chakra (Illus. 10) with the intent to clear any energy blockage in the Aura and Chakra. Then do the same for the animal. Visualize the white or golden sphere of light[27] in front of their 6th Chakra 12, inches out (Illus. 11), and after a few seconds visualize the sphere going through their Aura into their Chakra (Illus. 12) with the intent to clear the Aura and Chakra of any blockages. This clearing method should be used when you can't get up close with the animal, such as if the animal is in the wild, in a cage, in a barn, not friendly, in a tree, in water, etc.

The second method of clearing can be used if you are a Reiki Healer. You place one of your palms 12 inches away from your 6th Chakra and channel Reiki for 30 seconds through your Aura and into your Chakra with the intent to clear the Aura and Chakra of any blockages (Illus. 13). Do the same for the animal's 6th Chakra (Illus. 14), but you do not have to be within 12 inches of the animal's Chakra when channeling the Reiki. You can be any distance away as long as you can see the animal and are not closer than 12 inches to the Chakra. Both methods should only take 60 to 90 seconds to complete.

---

[26] By being 12 inches out you will be approximately in the Aura's Astral Layer and you will be assured you will be going through the Aura's Emotional and Mental Layers for clearing.

[27] The size of the sphere of light should be the size of the animal's 6th Chakra.

Visualize a white or golden sphere of light the size of your forehead in front of your 6th Chakra.

Illus. 9

69

Visualize the sphere going
through the Aura into your 6th Chakra.

Illus. 10

Visualize a white or golden sphere of light the size of the animal's forehead in front of their 6th Chakra.

Illus. 11

71

Visualize the sphere going through the Aura into the animal's 6th Chakra.

Illus. 12

Place one palm in front of the 6th Chakra and channel Reiki for 30 seconds through your Aura and into your 6th Chakra.

Illus. 13

73

Channel Reiki into the 6th Chakra of the animal for 30 seconds.

Illus. 14

Enter the Zone

The next step is entering the Zone. The Zone is a mental state where you shut out all unnecessary thoughts, distractions, and noise so you can concentrate on the task at hand. In this case, the task would be completing the next steps in communicating psychically with an animal. Every person has entered into this mental state of being oblivious to external noise and surrounding activities while concentrating on what they were doing at the time. Here are a few examples to give you a reference:

➢ Reading a book

➢ Watching a favorite TV show

➢ Studying for a test

➢ Playing a game

➢ On the computer

➢ Nature walk or hiking

➢ Doing a hobby

The key to this step is the ability to enter the Zone at will, within 30-60 seconds. If you meditate, practice self-hypnosis, or are a Reiki Healer, you are accustomed to entering the Zone when needed, so this step will not be a challenge for you. If you have your own method of entering the Zone, you are welcome to use it. If not, here is a simple, well known, but extremely effective technique you can use.

Start this technique by saying the word "Zone" silently to yourself. Over time, just saying the word "Zone" will program your subconscious mind to enter your Zone automatically without having to do anything consciously. Ultimately that is what you want to achieve, the ability to enter your Zone within seconds by just silently stating the word.

After saying "Zone" with eyes open, take a semi-deep breath (this is between a normal breath and a deep breath) and hold it for a few seconds. While you are holding your breath, simultaneously tense (tighten) your whole body as best you can. When you exhale the breath a few seconds later, stop tensing your body. Do this two more times and then resume normal breathing.

Next, you need to clear your mind of any thoughts and worries that do not pertain to your task at hand – psychically communicating with an animal. To do this, visualize holding a string tied to a helium balloon outside your body, then mentally place all the thoughts and worries you may have into the balloon and let go of the string so the balloon floats away. The balloon should be big enough to hold all the thoughts and worries you place in it.

If it's easier for you, give your thoughts and worries shape and color, then place them into a balloon. Once you have released the balloon and it starts to float away, start the next step.

There are a few options you can use to modify this technique. Instead of using a helium balloon, you can use a bubble, a basket with a hot air balloon attached, or a box next to you with a lid to close after you place the thoughts and worries into it.

You need to be able to enter the Zone standing up or sitting down in any environment, depending on your circumstances with the animal. So practice the technique both ways.

Visualize

Now that you are in the Zone, mentally visualize the information you want to send to the animal into an image or images. As in the example used in the Connect step, you want your dog to learn to use a new dog door - visualize an image or images of the dog going through the door (Illus. 15).

For beginners it is best to stick with information you can visualize into one image. As you become more experienced with this step, the information can be more in depth and you can visualize multiple images, like a slide show or short movie. Always keep the image or images clear and concise. This step should not take longer than a few minutes to complete.

Send Information

This step is sending the information you have visualized to the animal's Biological Intelligence. The 6th Chakra is the portal to the Biological Intelligence in all animals, so

Visualize the information you want
to send to the animal into an image or images.

Illus. 15

you are going to send what you have visualized through the animal's Aura into its 6th Chakra. There are two methods to accomplish this step. The first method: Visualize a funnel of white or golden light from your 6th Chakra going through your Aura and connecting to the animal's 6th Chakra through its Aura (Illus. 16). Once this is done, use your intent to send the visualized image(s) through the funnel of light into the animal's 6th Chakra and reaching their Biological Intelligence (Illus. 17). This should only take 15 to 30 seconds. The second method is to project the image(s) into the animal's 6th Chakra. Projecting is sending the image or images with your intent knowing they will go into the 6th Chakra reaching their Biological Intelligence instantly.

If your objective is only to send information and does not require a response from the animal, close the communication using the last step.

Receive Information

This is the most challenging step because it has several parts and psychic abilities come into play. The more you perform this step, the easier it will be for your psychic abilities to open and become stronger. You can put yourself on the fast track in opening and increasing all the Psychic abilities needed in this step by taking the Reiki Psychic Attunements[28]. As a side note, you do not have to be a Reiki Healer to take the Psychic Attunements; any person of any level of education or experience can take these Attunements.

---

[28] The Reiki Psychic Attunements are on the DVDs "Open and Expand your Psychic Abilities" Vols. 1 and 2.

Visualize a funnel of white or golden light from your 6th Chakra and connecting to the animal's 6th Chakra.

Illus. 16

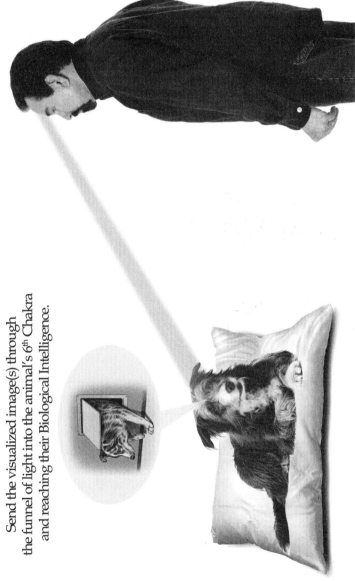

Send the visualized image(s) through the funnel of light into the animal's 6th Chakra and reaching their Biological Intelligence.

Illus. 17

81

In this step, you access the animal's Biological Intelligence through their Aura and 6th Chakra to receive information, not to send. The information you receive can be anything that's going on in the animal's life. This can include its health, pain, desires, fears, what it would like to do, etc. The information can be from the animal's past or a response to information just sent.

This information arrives in the form of Clairvoyance (mental images), Clairsentience (feelings, knowing, body sensations, and/or smells) or Clairaudience (sound). It might also arrive in a combination of two or all three psychic abilities. How you psychically receive the information will be unique for you and this depends on how your psychic abilities develop.

Here's how to receive information: Just like in sending information, you visualize a funnel of golden or white light from your 6th Chakra through your Aura connecting to the animal's 6th Chakra through its Aura (Illus. 18). Once this is done, you shift into a receptive mental mode with the intent that all information the animal desires or should send will flow through the funnel of light into your 6th Chakra and reach your Biological Intelligence. "Should send" are the keywords in your intent. This ensures that you will receive any information pertaining to any health or survival issues the animal has, even if the animal has reasons for you not to receive it. For example, an animal does not send information about it being abused (for fear of more abuse once the past abuse is exposed), or

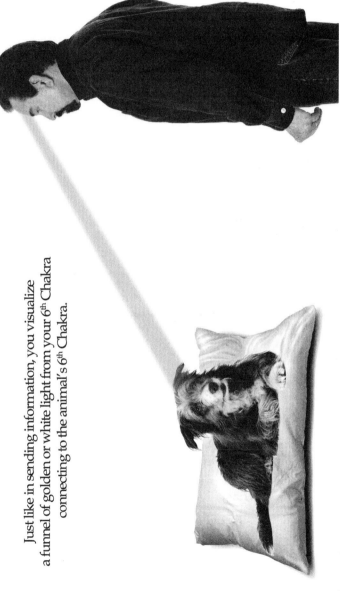

Just like in sending information, you visualize a funnel of golden or white light from your 6th Chakra connecting to the animal's 6th Chakra.

Illus. 18

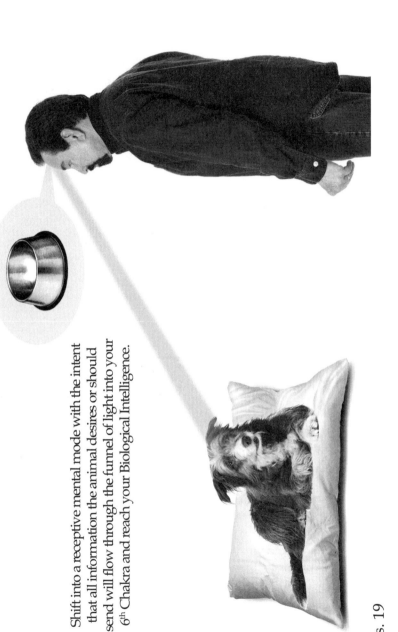

Shift into a receptive mental mode with the intent that all information the animal desires or should send will flow through the funnel of light into your 6th Chakra and reach your Biological Intelligence.

Illus. 19

information about a stomach problem (because of the fear of going to the veterinarian for treatment). Both examples relate to a survival and health issue, so you will receive the information.

Once you receive the psychic information, act upon it yourself, convey it to another person or persons so they can act upon it, or send information as a response to the information received. For example, you receive an image of an empty water bowl (Illus. 19), which means the dog is dehydrated and thirsty. You would then act upon the information by giving the dog water, or telling the person responsible for the dog it needs water quickly, or sending information back to the dog letting it know you will be getting it some water.

Here's an advanced method to receive information you can use when you feel ready. In this method you do not visualize a funnel or beam of light. Instead, shift into a receptive mental mode and use the intent that all information the animal wants or should send to you will flow into your 6th Chakra and Aura and appear in your Biological Intelligence instantly.

Ending Communication

Ending the communication with the animal is very easy. Once you are finished communicating, in your own words, mentally thank the animal for the experience (Illus. 20). You can also send a blessing.

Mentally thank the animal for the experience. You can also send a blessing.

Illus. 20

86

Non-Psychic Communication

There are several reasons why you will not receive information from an animal with which you are trying to communicate. It could be the animal just does not want to communicate with you at that point in time and/or does not have health or survival issues. But, the primary reason for an unsuccessful Animal Psychic Communication is that the person who is trying to communicate with the animal is too inexperienced to be able to perceive the information that the animal is sending. This problem is easily remedied by practicing the steps set forth in this book.

Long Distance

You can psychically communicate with any animal over long distance using the same steps. To do this you need to have a description of the animal. If you know or have met the animal, you are all set. If not, a photo of the animal helps, but is not required. Just get as many details (species, color, sex, location, etc.) as you can so you have a mental image of the animal to visualize during the steps. Once you have a mental image of the animal, visualize it being in front of you and perform the steps[29] as though the animal was actually there.

---

[29] If you are a Reiki Healer you can activate the Reiki Long Distance Symbol next to you and this will help with the long distance communication.

And God took a handful of southernly wind, blew His breath over it and created the horse.

- Bedouin Legend

Steps Recapped

9

Here's a recap of the steps without the detailed explanations. I recommend making a copy of them. This way you can have the steps close by for reference if needed during your first animal communications. Once you are experienced in performing the steps, you will be able to communicate with an animal in any environment or circumstance within five to seven minutes.

Connect

Be in an area with an animal you can see and would like to communicate with. Decide what information you want to send to the animal, then state this to yourself silently, using your own wording.

Chakra and Aura Clearing

Clear the first four layers of your Aura and 6th Chakra and the first four layers of the animal's Aura and 6th Chakra. Use the Sphere or Reiki method.

Enter the Zone

State the word "Zone" silently and use one of my methods or your own method to enter the Zone. If you are programmed to enter the Zone instantly, a method is not needed after you state the word "Zone."

Visualize

Mentally visualize the information you want to convey to the animal into an image or images.

Send Information

Visualize a funnel of white or golden light from your 6th Chakra through your Aura connecting to the animal's 6th Chakra through its Aura. Once this is done, use your intent to send the visualized image(s) through the funnel of light into the animal's 6th Chakra and reaching their Biological Intelligence. Or use the advanced method of projecting an image or images into the animal's Biological Intelligence.

Receive Information

Visualize a funnel of white or golden light connecting from your 6th Chakra through your Aura, to the animal's 6th Chakra through its Aura. Shift into a receptive mental mode with the intent that all information the animal wants or needs to send will flow through the funnel to your 6th Chakra into your Biological Intelligence. Or, use the advanced method. Do not visualize a funnel; just use the intent that all information the animal wants or needs to send will flow into your 6th Chakra and appear in your Biological Intelligence instantly.

End Connection

End the communication by mentally thanking the animal for the experience. As an option, you can also send a blessing.

Until one has loved an animal, a part of one's soul remains unawakened.

- Anatole France

Guidelines

10

Unfortunately, there are no shortcuts in developing the abilities needed in the steps of Animal Psychic Communication, but if you have patience and keep practicing with different animals in various circumstances, you will ultimately become proficient. Next are a few guidelines to help in your learning process.

- Do not have excess caffeine, alcohol, and/or drugs in your body when attempting to psychically communicate with animals for this will impair any communication.

- If you do not meditate now, learn how and meditate regularly. This will help develop the psychic abilities needed in the steps.

- Don't force communication, let it flow. If you sense it is not a good time to connect to the animal for any reason, try again later.

- Any type of communication can be misinterpreted. If this happens, don't dwell upon it - just try again with the intention to get it right.

- Intent is a very important part of Psychic Animal Communication, so mentally make your intent crystal clear during each step of the process.

- Animals do not have to show an interest in communicating or even look at you for you to successfully communicate with them.

- When you visualize information you want to send, make sure it is clear and concise and tells the story of the information you want to send. Otherwise, the animal will not be able to understand it.

- When sending more than one image, send them all at once with no pauses in between. This will enable the animal to understand what was sent and not get confused.

- If you are new at visualizing, practice as much as you can. Go to a quiet place, sit down and visualize your favorite movie scenes, the headlines of a newspaper, or practice visualizing information you might be sending to an animal in the future.

- If, on occasion, you experience an exceptionally busy mind and/or feel emotionally drained, do not attempt any Animal Psychic Communication because this will lower the chances of a successful communication. Just wait until you feel better.

- Any time you send information, you have the option to receive information back. This can manifest into a back and forth psychic conversation with the animal. This is the same with receiving information first. You might want to send information after you receive it. This can also manifest into a back and forth psychic conversation with the animal.

Love the animals: God has given them the rudiments of thought and joy untroubled.

- Fyodor Dostoyevsky

Reiki Pet Healing

If you have men who will exclude any of God's creatures from the shelter of compassion and pity, you will have men who will deal likewise with their fellow men.

- St. Francis of Assisi

Reiki

11

In this segment of the book I will assume you are a Reiki[30] Healer or at least know the basic teachings and fundamentals of Reiki. If this is not the case and you would like to learn about Reiki and/or are interested in becoming a Reiki Healer, you can do so with my Reiki DVDs and

---

[30] Reiki, pronounced "Ray-key" comes from the Japanese words "rei" meaning spirit and "ki" meaning energy. It is usually translated as "universal life energy."

Reiki books. Another option would be to find a local Reiki Master and take Reiki Attunements and classes. Any person with a desire to help animals can learn Reiki. If you are new to Reiki, it should be noted that Reiki does not cause stress, discomfort, pain, or any harm whatsoever to the pet or the Healer.

Reiki Healing

How Reiki can help with pets:

* Reduce symptoms from illness and disease.

* Provide comfort and relief for symptoms that develop from an illness or disease.

* Pain relief from an injury or illness.

* Accelerating the healing of an injury or surgery.

* Pain relief from arthritis and joint-related problems.

* Releasing stress, fear, anxiety, and anger.

* Maintaining the health of animals that are healthy.

Reiki can produce sudden and dramatic changes, but most of the time Reiki Healing is a process, especially with health conditions in animals that have developed over time.

Reiki Caveat

At the beginning of the book I stated the following, but I feel it's very important to mention it again before I start giving instructions on Reiki pet healing. Reiki is only to be used in conjunction with, not in place of, veterinary medicine. Always take your pet to a veterinarian when you first suspect illness or disease. In fact, the diagnosis you receive from the veterinarian will be used in my method of Reiki pet healing.

The purity of a person's heart can be quickly measured by how they regard animals.

- Anonymous

Chakra Attunements

12

I use Chakra Attunements in my method of Reiki pet healing. A Chakra Attunement works directly with the animal's Chakra that is affected by a physical ailment or disease which has manifested and/or is located in that Chakra's Area of Influence. Or, if there is a health challenge in a body system, you work with the Chakra responsible for that system. During the Attunement you will use intent and Reiki Symbols while channeling (sending) Reiki through the four layers of the Aura and into a Chakra. Once this is done, the Reiki is processed by the Chakra to help with the health challenge and then it flows through the rest of the Chakra system. The Attunement is effective because it focuses primarily on the Chakra's Area of Influence where the health challenge is located.

Area of Influence

The knowledge of the Area of Influence for each Chakra is a very important element in a Chakra Attunement. To give guidance with this there are Chakra locations and Areas of Influence illustrations at the end of the book. You will use the illustration that matches the pet you will be performing the Attunement on to determine the Chakra to use during the Attunement. Pets come in all shapes and sizes and you will have to gauge the Chakra's Area of Influence to scale on the pet you will be healing. If the species of pet is not represented in an illustration, use the one that most closely resembles their body structure to give you a reference in finding the locations and Areas of Influence for their major Chakras.

Before you use an Area of Influence illustration, you must first identify the specific physical ailment or disease and where it is located in the pet's body. Once this is done, you will use an illustration to see which Chakra's Area of Influence the physical ailment or disease is in and that will be the Chakra to use during the Attunement.

A broken leg, bruise, broken tooth, or cut, etc. are pretty straightforward when determining what Chakra's Area of Influence these injuries are located. Just look at the illustration of the pet and see in which Chakra's Area of Influence the injury is located in and that will be the Chakra to use during the Attunement.

The majority of the time you will use the information from a veterinarian's diagnosis (such as a heart problem, a kidney problem, a thyroid problem, etc.) to decide what Chakras to use in the Attunement. You will need to ask the veterinarian for the location in your pet's body of the health problem. For example, if there was a kidney infection, ask the veterinarian, "Where are the kidneys located in my pet's body?" With this information, refer to the Chakra illustration at the back of the book that shows the Areas of Influence of the pet's Chakras. The Chakra's Area of Influence where your pet's kidneys are located will be the Chakra you will use during the Attunement.

However, a physical ailment or disease sometimes is not localized, but is manifested throughout a body system. If this is the case, you will still need a veterinarian's diagnosis and then ask the veterinarian which body system the heath challenge is in. When this happens, use the guidelines below to decide what Chakra to use during the Attunement.

- Muscular System: Use the 1st Chakra.

- Skeletal System: Use the 1st Chakra.

- Endocrine System: Use the 3rd Chakra.

- Nervous System: Use the 6th Chakra.

- Reproductive System: Use the 2nd Chakra.

- Urinary System: Use the 3rd Chakra.

- Digestive System: Use the 2nd Chakra.

- Respiratory System: Use the 5th Chakra.

- Cardiovascular System: Use the 4th Chakra.

- Lymphatic/Immune System: Use the 2nd Chakra.

- Colds or Viruses: Use the 4th Chakra.

- Blood Specific Illness: Use the 4th Chakra.

If the same ailment or disease has manifested in more than one location in the body (e.g., arthritis, tumors, muscle spasms, skin problems) you can perform a separate Attunement for each location. Another option would be to use the body system where the root cause of the ailment or disease has manifested[31] and perform one Attunement[32]. A few examples of this might include:

- Muscle spasms throughout the body: you would use the 1st Chakra, which is responsible for the Muscular System.

---

[31] You would need the help of a veterinarian to determine this type of information.

[32] In health challenges like this, you have to decide what is best for the pet, multiple Attunements or one Attunement.

- Arthritis in multiple locations: you would use the 2nd Chakra, which is responsible for the Immune System.

- Multiple joint problems: you would use the 1st Chakra, which is responsible for the Skeletal System.

Psychic Information

You might receive psychic information from a pet indicating that a region in their body needs a Chakra Attunement. If that happens, determine which Chakra's Area of Influence the region is located in and that's the Chakra you will use for the Attunement.

We can judge the heart of a man by his treatment of animals.

- Immanual Kant

Step-By-Step

13

This chapter has the steps and explanations for performing a Reiki Chakra Attunement on a pet. If you notice the Reiki Symbols in the steps have variations or are completely different from the Reiki Symbols to which you have been attuned, don't worry. You can use your Reiki Symbols and they will be just as effective. Just make sure the symbols equate to the Power Symbol, Long Distance, and Mental/Emotional Symbol[33] used in the steps. The Reiki Master Symbol is not used in the steps. If you use a Reiki Master Symbol as part of your personal preparation before you give any Reiki Attunement or Reiki Healing, you can still do so before a Chakra Attunement.

Just like in the Animal Psychic Communication, you will be using your intent throughout the Chakra Attunement. Again, intent is the state of mind when you are focused on a specific purpose, a course of action. Unlike in Animal Psychic Communication where being in a quiet environment is not necessary, you should strive for having a quiet environment when giving a Chakra Attunement to a pet.

Several items should be noted now before you start on the steps. During the Chakra Attunement when you are channeling Reiki, you do not physically touch the pet and you are at least two feet away from the pet. In addition, I use only the back[34] Chakras during the Attunements and those are the Chakras I will describe during the steps. The reason for this is that with most non-human animals their back Chakras are the easiest to access because they do not walk upright and might be in a resting position during the Attunement. With Humans, usually the front Chakras are accessed and used during Chakra healing work because we do walk upright. Accessing the back side of a Chakra will have the same results as accessing the front side. If there are circumstances when you feel a need to use the front Chakra instead of the back Chakra and you have access to it, by all means use it.

---

[33] The four Reiki Symbols are described in the back of the book.

[34] Unless it is the 6th or 7th Chakras and they are located on the head.

The Steps

Step 1

Know the health issue the pet needs an Attunement for and determine what back Chakra to use during the Attunement for this health issue (Illus. 21). Use the instructions in Chapter Twelve for this step and the Chakra illustrations at the end of the book.

Step 2

Have the pet you are going to perform the Chakra Attunement on in their normal enclosure, even though they might be tame outside of it. The pet needs to be in their enclosure so you can access their Chakras without the pet moving away from you and interrupting the Attunement. Pets, especially small ones, usually have enclosures such as hutches, cages, aquariums, etc. Larger pets, such as horses, will have enclosures such as paddocks or corrals. The exception to this is dogs and cats because they usually do not have an enclosure. During a Chakra Attunement a dog or cat can be in their own bed, on the floor, or in their favorite area. However, if an enclosure (travel cage, dog run, training pen, etc.) is available for your dog or cat, I would recommend using it during the Attunement.

Step 3

Clear the area where the Attunement is going to be performed in case there is lingering Psychic Debris. There are two ways to accomplish this. The first way is to visualize or imagine white or golden light filling the

Know the health issue the pet needs an Attunement for and determine what back Chakra to use during the Attunement for this health issue.

Illus. 21

area with the intent to dissolve any Psychic Debris that is present (Illus. 22). Or, you can smudge[35] the area (Illus. 23) with the intent to dissolve any Psychic Debris that is present. There is more in-depth information about Psychic Debris in Step 12. This step should take about 30 seconds.

Step 4

The next step is grounding. Grounding ensures Reiki will flow strongly and uninterrupted through you during the Attunement. Reiki Healers usually have their own method for grounding, so if you have one, use it for this step or use the following method: Stand up. Take a deep breath and visualize golden light coming in from the top of your head (7th Chakra) and flowing through your body, out both legs and feet into the earth (Illus. 24). While it is flowing through your body, have the intent for this white or golden light to balance all of your Chakras. Then, take a deep breath, wait a few seconds, then bring the light back up from the earth, all the way back up both feet and legs and out the top of your head (7th Chakra) with the same intent to balance your Chakras. This should only take a few minutes. You will sense a feeling of well-being after the process is complete.

Step 5

Now that you are grounded, state the intent for the Chakra Attunement silently to yourself (Illus. 25). For example, if the pet has a kidney infection, state silently to yourself,

---

[35] Smudging is the burning of sage, cedar, and sweetgrass (although different herbs and incense can be used) to create smoke that can be used to cleanse and purify.

Visualize white or golden light filling the area with the intent to dissolve any Psychic Debris that is present.

Illus. 22

Smudge the area with
the intent to dissolve any
Psychic Debris that is present.

Illus. 23

115

Take a deep breath and visualize golden light coming in from the top of your head (7th Chakra) and flowing through your body, out both legs and feet into the earth.

Illus. 24

Now that you are grounded, state the intent for the Chakra Attunement silently to yourself.

Illus. 25

117

"The Chakra Attunement is to help heal Jet's [use the pet's name] kidney infection." Use your own wording, but make sure the intent for the Chakra Attunement is clear. As an option, at this time you can also ask your higher power, source, Guardian Angel(s), Reiki Guide(s), etc., for guidance during the Chakra Attunement.

Step 6

Steps 6 and 7 are performed in every Chakra Attunement to clear a mental and/or emotional blockage in the Aura or Chakra that might have manifested because of the pet's health issue. If there is a block and it is not cleared, this can slow down or prevent healing of the health issue.

Move into a position so you can access the pet's 7th Chakra. Visualize (Illus. 26) or draw[36] (Illus. 27) the Mental/ Emotional Symbol the size of the 7th Chakra about twelve inches in front of the 7th Chakra and activate it. Then, embed the symbol into the middle of the Chakra by visualizing (Illus. 28) or moving it there with your finger (Illus. 29).

If you need help to determine the location of the 7th Chakra in the pet you are performing an Attunement on, refer to the Chakra illustrations at the end of the book. If there isn't an illustration for the type of pet you are giving the Attunement to, use the illustration that has a similar body type to give you an idea of the pet's 7th Chakra location.

---

[36] Some people have a hard time visualizing Reiki Symbols, so they draw or trace them in the air, mentally or with a finger(s), where they want them to be.

Visualize the Mental/Emotional Symbol the size of the 7th Chakra about twelve inches in front of the 7th Chakra and activate it.

Illus. 26

119

Draw the Mental/Emotional Symbol the size of the 7th Chakra about twelve inches in front of the 7th Chakra and activate it.

Illus. 27

Visualize embedding the symbol into the middle of the Chakra.

Illus. 28

Embed the symbol into the Chakra by moving it there with your finger.

Illus. 29

122

Visualizing or drawing the symbol twelve inches out from the Chakra ensures it is in front of the Mental and Emotional Layers of the Aura.

When you activate a Reiki Symbol, it means you turn it on, make it work, put it into action, etc. There are many ways to activate a Reiki Symbol and it depends on the way you were taught or your preference. A few ways to activate a symbol include thinking of its name, saying it out loud, saying it silently if non-attuned Reiki people are present, or you can just use your intent to activate the symbol. When some Reiki Healers visualize a symbol, it's activated automatically with their intent.

Once you have the Reiki Symbol activated over the Chakra, the symbol is embedded into the center of the Chakra. You can embed the symbol several ways: visualize moving the symbol into the Chakra, or if you have drawn the symbol, move the symbol into the center of the Chakra with your finger. This step will take several minutes.

Step 7

After the symbol is embedded into the 7th Chakra, channel Reiki through the Aura into the center of the Chakra for a few minutes. Channel Reiki with the palms towards the Chakra. Your palms should be at least two feet away from the Chakra (Illus. 30). You can channel Reiki from as far away as you like, as long you can see the pet. Channel the Reiki with intent for it to clear any blocks in the Aura and Chakra associated with the health challenge for which the Attunement is being performed. You should channel Reiki for about three to five minutes.

Channel Reiki into the center of the 7th Chakra.

Illus. 30

124

Step 8

Move into a position where you can access the pet's Chakra you selected to use during the Attunement. In this example I'm working with the cat's 4th Chakra (Illus. 31), but if I was working with the cat's 2nd Chakra, I would need to move to the back of the cat (Illus. 32).

Now visualize (Illus. 33) or draw the Power Symbol (Illus. 34) about twelve inches in front of the Chakra, activate the symbol, and embed the symbol into the middle of the Chakra by visualizing (Illus. 35) or guide it there with your finger (Illus. 36).

By embedding the Power Symbol into the Chakra, you will increase the Reiki that will be channeled in Step 9. This step takes about thirty seconds.

Step 9

Next, stay in the same position and visualize (Illus. 37) or draw the Long Distance Symbol (Illus. 38) about twelve inches in front of the Chakra, activate the symbol, and embed the symbol into the middle of the Chakra by visualizing (Illus. 39) or moving it there with your finger (Illus. 40). By embedding the Long Distance Symbol into the Chakra, it will be there for present and future healing for the intent you channel in Step 10. This step takes about thirty seconds.

Move into a position where you can access the pet's Chakra you selected to use during the Attunement.

Illus. 31

Move to the back of the cat.

Illus. 32

127

Visualize the Power Symbol and activate it

Illus. 33

Draw the Power Symbol and activate it.

Illus. 34

129

Visualize embedding the Power Symbol into the middle of the Chakra.

Illus. 35

Embed the Power Symbol into the Chakra by moving it there with your finger.

Illus. 36

131

Visualize the Long Distance Symbol and activate it.

Illus. 37

Draw the Long Distance Symbol
and activate it.

楚气心

Illus. 38

133

Visualize embedding the Long Distance Symbol into the middle of the Chakra.

Illus. 39

Embed the Long Distance Symbol into the Chakra by moving it there with your finger.

Illus. 40

135

Step 10

The two Reiki Symbols are now embedded into the Chakra you have selected to use during the Attunement. Now, channel Reiki into the center of this Chakra (Illus. 41) with the intent for it to go into the Chakra and flow directly to the health issue for which the Attunement is given. Channel Reiki with your palms towards the center of the Chakra. Your palms should be a minimum of two feet away from the Chakra. Channel Reiki for about five minutes.

Step 11

The Attunement is now complete and you need to break your energy connection with the pet. Most Reiki Healers have a method to break this connection when ending a healing session or Attunement. If you have a method you use, feel free to use it. If not, thank the pet for cooperating during the Attunement and as an option, you can include a blessing (Illus. 42), then rub and shake your hands for a few seconds (Illus. 43) with the intent to break the energy connection with the pet.

Step 12

This last step is a precautionary step. It is clearing the area, yourself, and the pet of any Psychic Debris that might have been released by the pet during the Attunement.

Channel Reiki into the
center of the Chakra.

Illus. 41

137

Thank the pet for cooperating during the Attunement and as an option, you can include a blessing.

Illus. 42

Rub and shake your hands for a few seconds with the intent to break the energy connection with the pet.

Illus. 43

139

In all of my previous Reiki books and Reiki DVDs[37] I explain (in the context of people) that Psychic Debris[38] is negative emotions that have accumulated over a period of time (this can be years) in the Mental and Emotional Layers of the Aura because they were not processed and released by the individual. The emotions accumulated can be fear, grief, anger, hate, etc. If not removed, Psychic Debris can ultimately resonate down to the person's physical body and weaken their immune system, causing illness and disease. When you perform various Attunements (Chakra, Aura, Healing, Reiki Level, etc.) on a person or have healing sessions with a person, Psychic Debris is released from the Aura, which is what needs to happen as part of a successful healing process. The amount of Psychic Debris released varies, depending on the individual and his or her condition and circumstances.

Psychic Debris that is released during an Attunement or a healing session needs to be destroyed. If not, it can attach to the Aura of the person giving the Attunement or healing session or linger in the room and attach itself to another person or animal that enters the room in the future. When lingering Psychic Debris attaches to your Aura, you can experience the same symptoms that created it and even the health problems it has manifested. This is why Reiki Healers who do not clear themselves after an Attunement or healing session can sometimes feel emotionally drained or sick and experience strange emotions to which they are unaccustomed.

---

[37] I have a DVD trilogy: Remove Psychic Debris & Heal.

[38] Psychic Debris is called different names by Healers, such as "negative thought forms" and "emotional or mental blocks."

Pets can also have Psychic Debris which can be released during a Chakra Attunement with the chance of it attaching to the Human Aura, and this can cause unforeseen health problems. Or, if the Psychic Debris lingers in the area, it can become attached to another pet's Aura in the future and cause problems for that pet.

If you think that it is not possible for Human Psychic Debris and Pet Psychic Debris to cross-contaminate each other's Aura, then consider this: This same scenario plays out in the physical world with viruses. Viruses can become contaminated with genetic materials from different animals. This makes it possible for the virus to infect all the animals from which it has acquired the genetic materials. For example, a bird and a Human can be infected by the same virus that has genetic materials from both and transmit the virus back and forth to each other. I believe a quick clearing of any possible Psychic Debris released by the pet is smart and can prevent future health problems for you, the pet, other pets, and other people.

If your pet does release Psychic Debris during the Chakra Attunement, there is really nothing to fear because it is easily destroyed. For this final step, use one of the methods for clearing Psychic Debris described in Step 3 with a modified intent. Your intent will be to dissolve any Psychic Debris that was released during the Chakra Attunement.

Long Distance Attunement

You can give a Chakra Attunement to a pet over long distance using the same steps. To do this, just visualize the pet in front of you and perform the steps like the pet was actually there. Visualizing the pet should not be a problem since you most likely know the pet. If the Chakra Attunement is for a pet you do not know, refer to the long distance segment at the end of Chapter 8 for the information needed to visualize a pet in this circumstance. As an option, you can activate the Reiki Long Distance Symbol next to you and this will help with the long distance Chakra Attunement.

**Our perfect companions never have
fewer than four feet.**

\- Colette

A house is not a home without a pet.

- Anonymous

Steps Recapped

14

This chapter is a recap of the Chakra Attunement steps without the detailed explanations and illustrations. Review the steps a few times before you perform your first Chakra Attunement. It is a good idea to make a copy of the condensed steps so you will have a reference if needed when giving your first Chakra Attunements.

Step 1

Know the health issue your pet needs an Attunement for and determine what back Chakra to use during the Attunement for this health issue.

Step 2

Have the pet in their enclosure. A dog or cat can be in their own bed, on the floor, or in their favorite area.

Step 3

Clear the area where the Attunement is going to be performed of any Psychic Debris. Visualize or imagine white or golden light filling the area with the intent to dissolve any Psychic Debris that is present. Or, smudge the area with the intent to dissolve any Psychic Debris that is present.

Step 4

Ground yourself with the golden light coming in from the top of your head (7th Chakra) and flowing through your body, out both legs and feet into the earth, and back up again out the top of your head with the intent to balance your Chakras.

Step 5

State the intent for the Chakra Attunement silently to yourself. As an option, you can also ask your higher power, source, Guardian Angel(s), Reiki Guide(s), etc., for guidance during the Chakra Attunement.

Step 6

Move into a position from which you can access the pet's 7th Chakra. Visualize or draw the Mental/Emotional Symbol about twelve inches in front of the pet's 7th Chakra and activate it, then embed the symbol into the middle of the 7th Chakra.

Step 7

Now that the symbol is embedded into the 7th Chakra, channel Reiki through the Aura into the center of the Chakra from a minimum of two feet away for three to five minutes. Channel Reiki with the intent for it to clear any blocks in the Aura and Chakra associated with the health challenge for which the Attunement is being performed.

Step 8

Move into a position where you can access the pet's back Chakra you have decided to use during the Attunement. Now visualize or draw the Power Symbol about twelve inches in front of it, activate the symbol, and embed it into the center of the Chakra.

Step 9

Next, stay in the same position and visualize or draw the Long Distance Symbol about twelve inches in front of the same Chakra, activate the symbol, and embed it into the center of the Chakra.

Step 10

Now, channel Reiki from a minimum of two feet away into the center of the same back Chakra with the intent for the Reiki to go into the Chakra and flow directly to the health issue for which the Attunement is being given.

Step 11

The Attunement is now complete and you need to break your energy connection with the pet. Thank the pet for cooperating during the Attunement. You can include a blessing if you wish, then rub and shake your hands for a few seconds with the intent to break the energy connection.

Step 12

Clear the area of any Psychic Debris that the pet might have released during the Attunement using one of the methods from Step 3 with a modified intent. Your intent will be to dissolve any Psychic Debris that was released during the Chakra Attunement.

If having a soul means being able to feel love and loyalty and gratitude, then animals are better off than a lot of humans.

- James Herriot

A dog is the only thing on earth that will love you more than you love yourself.

- Josh Billings

Guidelines

15

Here are additional guidelines for performing a Chakra Attunement. You should review all of them before giving your first Chakra Attunement to a pet.

Guidelines

- Do as many of the following suggestions as possible before giving a Chakra Attunement. By doing so, this will keep your focus sharper during the Attunement. Limit or stop eating all animal protein 12 hours before the Attunement. Consume only water or juice four to six hours before the Attunement. Limit or stop use of caffeine drinks four to six hours before the Attunement. Stop drinking alcohol 12 hours before the Attunement. Limit sugar 12 hours before the Attunement. Limit or stop smoking four to six hours before the Attunement.

- Remember the size of the symbols you visualize will be based on the size of the pet's Chakra.

- Before performing a Chakra Attunement, if time permits, psychically communicate with the pet to let it know what is going to happen.

- Maintain strong intent and focus throughout the entire Chakra Attunement.

- During a Chakra Attunement talk only when necessary so you will not be distracted.

- Pets can feel very relaxed after a Chakra Attunement and will often fall asleep during the session. If that happens, continue the Attunement until it is completed.

- Once you become experienced with performing a Chakra Attunement, it should never last longer than fifteen minutes. Of course, there are always exceptions to this and you will know intuitively when an Attunement needs to be longer.

- When channeling Reiki into a Chakra during the Attunement you can use one or two palms.

- Let the pet take it easy for at least a few hours after the Attunement to allow the Reiki to filter throughout the pet's entire Chakra System.

- After the pet receives the Chakra Attunement it can become dehydrated. Make sure the pet has access to plenty of water. The pet can also experience increased elimination for a brief period after the Chakra Attunement.

- For minor health problems, one or two Chakra Attunements will suffice. Serious or chronic health challenges will need additional Chakra Attunements. How many will depend on your judgment since you will be monitoring the situation. There is no danger to an animal of having too many Chakra Attunements.

- Review the Chakra Attunement steps a few times before you actually perform your first Attunement.

- Reiki Chakra Attunements are usually only for pets, but an Attunement can be performed on an animal in the wild, but only if circumstances permit it and you are in a safe position.

- While performing a Chakra Attunement, you might feel sensations of heat, cold, or vibrations in your palms. If this happens, do not worry. It is part of the Attunement process. Some people do not experience any sensations while performing a Chakra Attunement, but the Attunement is still given successfully.

- If the location where a health challenge has manifested overlaps into two Chakras' Areas of Influence, use the Area of Influence that contains the majority of the health challenge. Or, if you intuitively feel it is necessary, perform a Chakra Attunement on both of the Chakras.

Chakra Balancing

In closing, I would like to mention Chakra Balancing. Chakra Balancing is a fast and simple way to maintain the health of a pet once it is healthy and it only takes seven minutes. Here's how to perform Chakra Balancing:

Start with the pet's 7th Chakra and channel Reiki into it for about a minute with the intent for the Reiki to go into the Chakra and balance it and then flow through the rest of the pet's body. You then do the same for each of the remaining six Major Chakras.

154

If it is possible during Chakra Balancing, place your hands directly on the pet's Chakras when channeling Reiki, as this will strengthen your bond with the pet. If this is not possible, you can channel Reiki from a distance into the Chakras.

There is nothing in which the birds differ more from man than the way in which they can build and yet leave a landscape as it was before.

- Robert Lynd

Chakra Illustrations

The next pages have illustrations of the seven Major Chakra locations and Areas of Influence for each Chakra for various animals. Chakras one through five in the illustrations are reflected on the back[39] of the animal, which are the locations you will work with in my teachings.

---

[39] If you need to know the location of the front side of a Chakra, it would be parallel and vertical with the back Chakra, except, of course, on the front side.

Use the illustration that matches the animal you are working with when you need a Chakra's location and/or a Chakra's Area of Influence.

As I mentioned earlier, animals come in all shapes and sizes. This means you will have to gauge a Chakra's location and its Area of Influence to scale on the animal you will be psychically communicating with or performing a Chakra Attunement on.

You might find the species of animal you are working with is not represented in an illustration. If this happens, use the illustration that most closely resembles their body structure to give you a point of reference in locating a Chakra's location, and its Area of Influence.

I have included three illustrations of invertebrates that will show you a point of reference if you ever work with an invertebrate.

Vertebrate Illustrations

- Dog (Illus. 44)
- Cat (Illus. 45)
- Fish (Illus. 46)
- Horse (Illus. 47)
- Bird (Illus. 48)
- Rabbit (Illus. 49)
- Snake (Illus. 50)
- Mouse (Illus. 51)
- Ferret (Illus. 52)
- Tortoise (Illus. 53)
- Lizard (Illus. 54)

- Frog (Illus. 55)
- Goat (Illus. 56)
- Pig (Illus. 57)
- Cock (Illus. 58)
- Sheep (Illus. 59)
- Duck (Illus. 60)
- Cow (Illus. 61)
- Hamster (Illus. 62)

Invertebrate Illustrations

- Tarantula (Illus. 63)
- Bee (Illus. 64)
- Ant (Illus. 65)

Chakra Illustration Legend

🌀	= Chakra location
Shaded area	= Area of Influence of the Chakra

A1 = 1st Chakra's Area of Influence
A2 = 2nd Chakra's Area of Influence
A3 = 3rd Chakra's Area of Influence
A4 = 4th Chakra's Area of Influence
A5 = 5th Chakra's Area of Influence
A6 = 6th Chakra's Area of Influence
A7 = 7th Chakra's Area of Influence

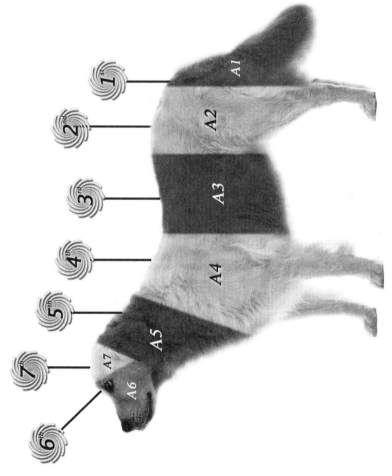

(Illus. 44) Dog

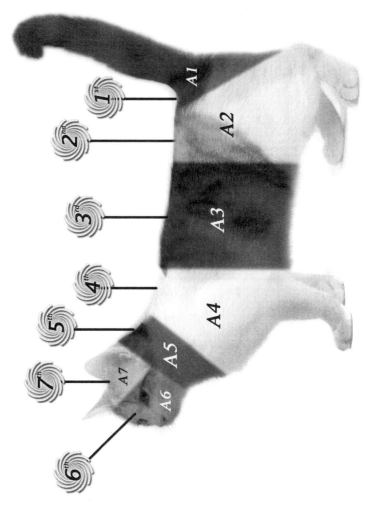

(Illus. 45) Cat

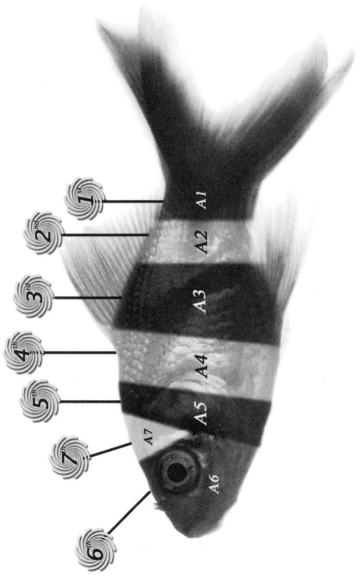

(Illus. 46) Fish

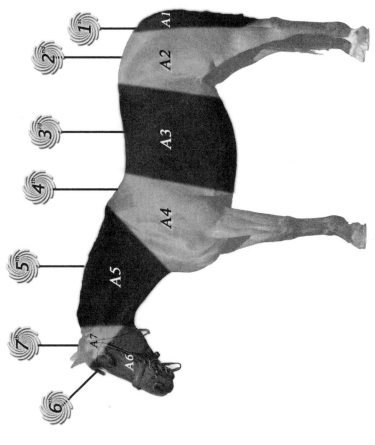

(Illus. 47) Horse

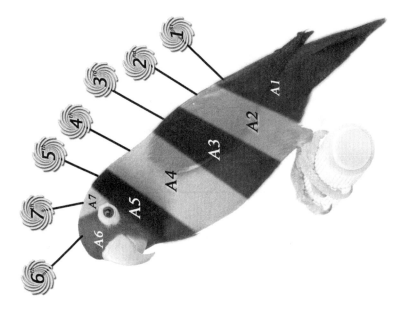

(Illus. 48) Bird

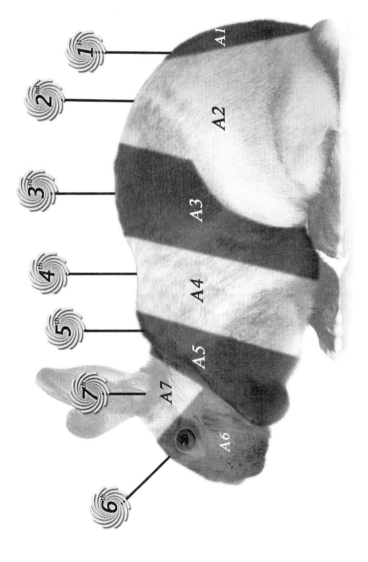

(Illus. 49) Rabbit

165

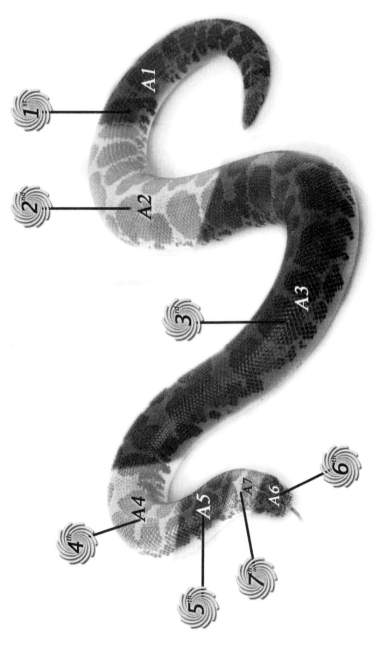

(Illus. 50) Snake

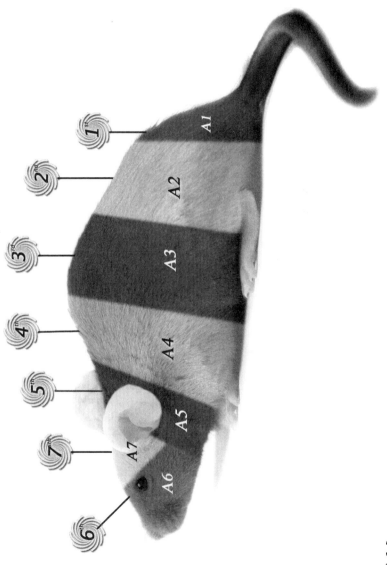

(Illus. 51) Mouse

167

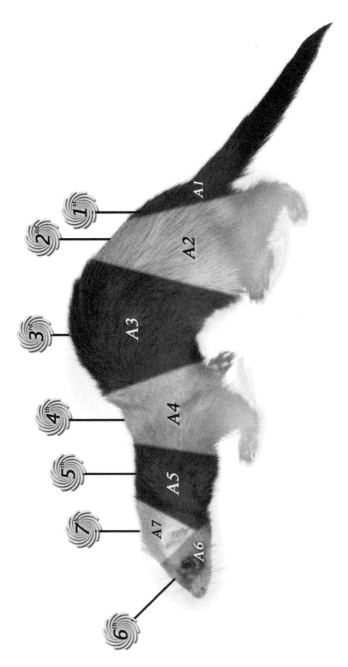

(Illus. 52) Ferret

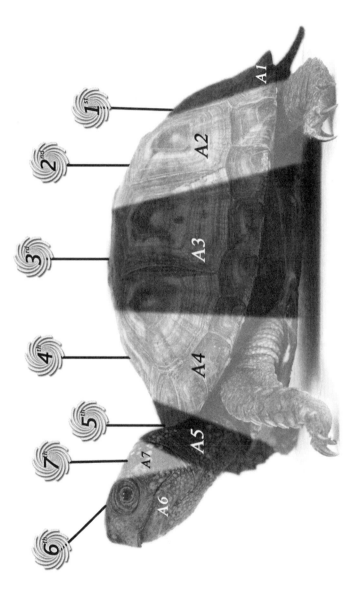

(Illus. 53) Tortoise

169

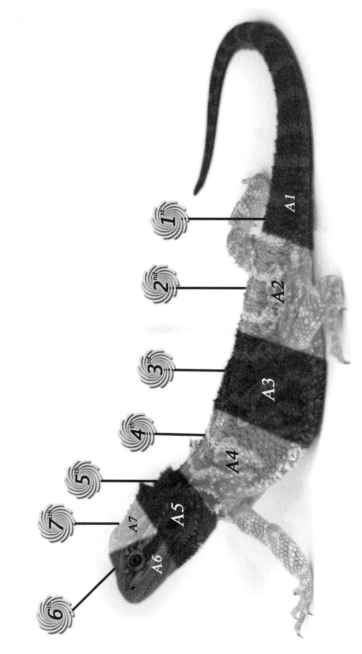

(Illus. 54) Lizard

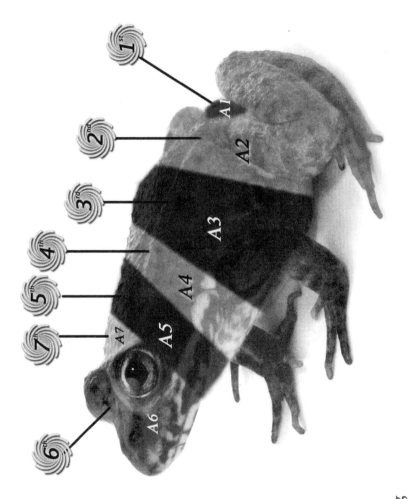

(Illus. 55) Frog

171

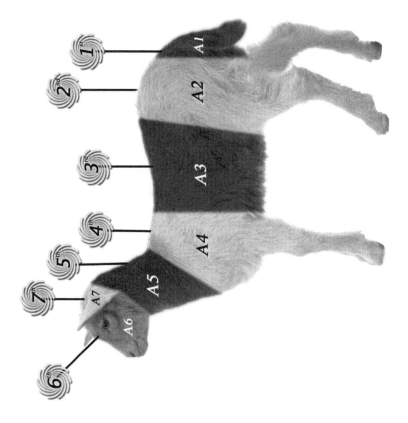

(Illus. 56) Goat

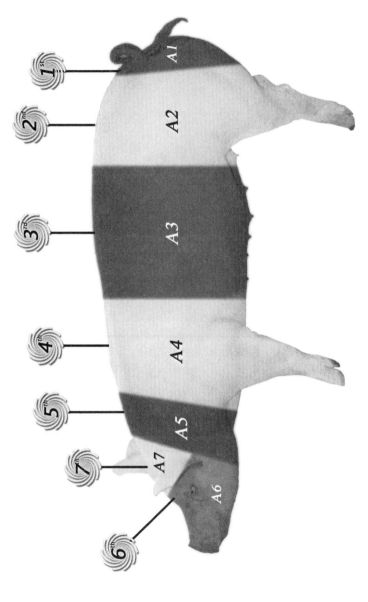

(Illus. 57) Pig

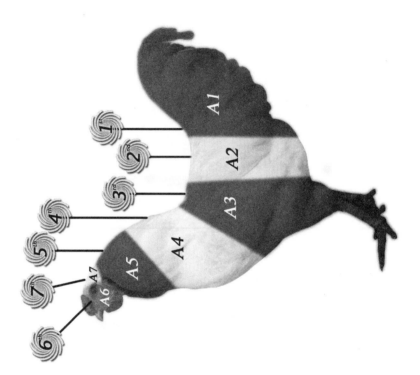

(Illus. 58) Cock

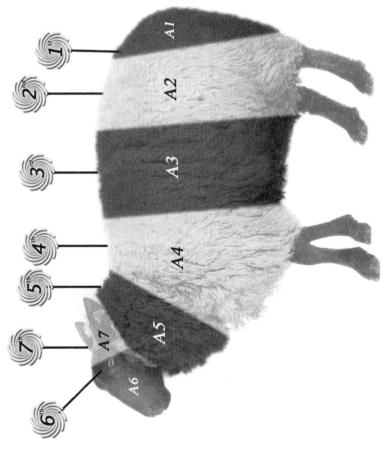

(Illus. 59) Sheep

175

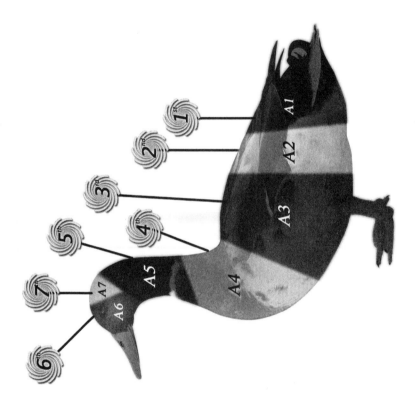

(Illus. 60) Duck

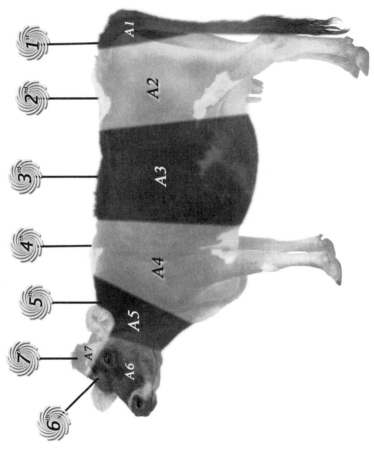

(Illus. 61) Cow

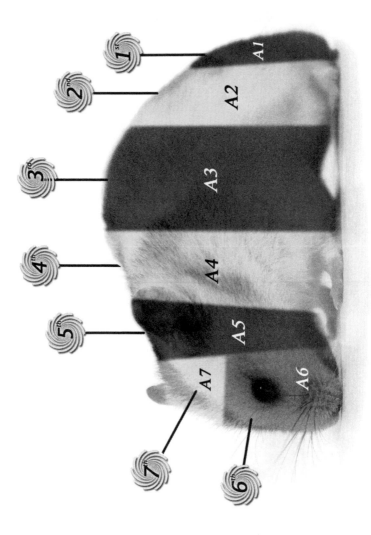

(Illus. 62) Hamster

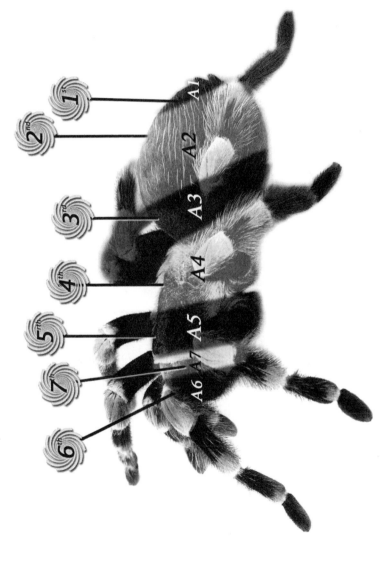

(Illus. 63) Tarantula

179

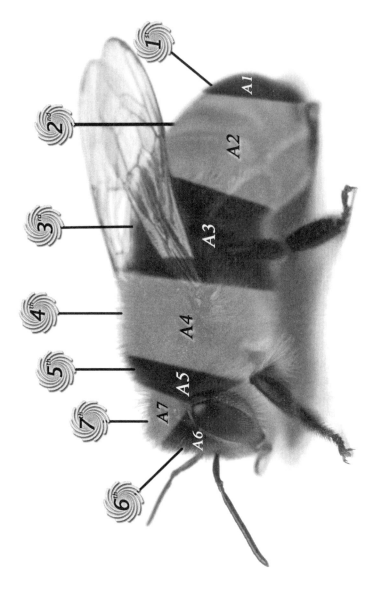

(Illus. 64) Bee

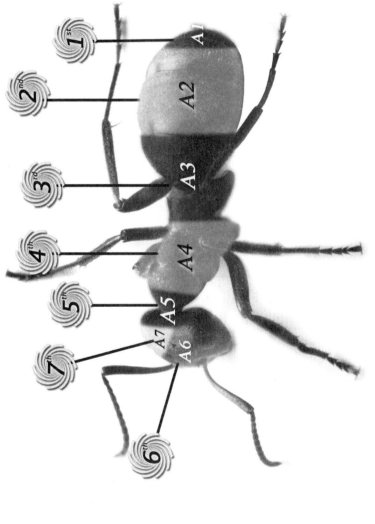

(Illus. 65) Ant

181

Reiki Symbols

Cho Ku Rei

The Usui Power Symbol. It is also called the "Power Increase" Symbol. Its name is *Cho Ku Rei*, which means, *Put all the power in the universe here.* The Power Symbol has many uses when activated, but it is primarily used to increase the power of Reiki or to focus Reiki on a specific location, and also for protection.

Reiki Symbols

Hon Sha Ze Sho Nen

The Usui Long Distance Symbol. It is also referred to as the "Long Distance" and the "Absentee" Symbol. Its name is *Hon Sha Ze Sho Nen*. When activated with specific intent, Reiki can be sent anywhere, anytime in the past, present, or future. Distance, time, and space are not a barrier when you use this symbol.

Reiki Symbols

Sei He Ki

The Usui Mental/Emotional Symbol. It is also called the "Mental" or "Mental/Emotional/Addiction" Symbol. Its name is *Sei He Ki* and it means, *God and humanity become one.* This symbol has many uses when activated, but is commonly used in emotional, mental, and addictive healing situations.

Reiki Symbols

Dai Koo Myo

The Usui Reiki Master Symbol. Its name is *Dai Koo Myo*. The Master Symbol is the ultimate Reiki Symbol in all aspects. It intensifies Reiki, takes it to a higher level. When you activate other Reiki Symbols with the Master Symbol, the symbols are then taken to their highest level of effectiveness.

Index

Bibliography

Anodea, Judith. Wheels of Life: A User's Guide to the Chakra System. Llewellyn Publications, 1999. ISBN-13: 978-0875423203.

Davies, Brenda. The 7 Healing Chakras Workbook. Ulysses Press, 2003. ISBN-13: 978-1569753675.

Friedlander, John and Hemsher, Gloria. Basic Psychic Development: A User's Guide to Auras, Chakra & Clairvoyance. Weiser Books, 1999. ISBN-13: 978-1578630233.

Hewitt, William W. Psychic Development for Beginners: An Easy Guide to Releasing and Developing Your Psychic Abilities. Llewellyn Publications, 1996. ISBN-13: 978-1567183603.

Martin, Ann. Food Pets Die For: Shocking Facts About Pet Food. NewSage Press 2008. ISBN-10: 0939165562.

Pond, David. Chakras for Beginners: Honor Your Energy. Llewellyn Publications, 1999. ISBN-13: 978-1567185379.

Ranquet, Joan. Communication With All Life. Hay House 2007. ISBN-13: 978-4401916817.

Redmond, Layne. Chakra Meditation: Transformation through the Seven Energy Centers of the Body. Sounds True, 2004. ISBN-13: 978-1591791782.

Sanders, Pete A. You Are Psychic!: The Free Soul Method. Fireside, 1999. ISBN-13: 978-0684857046.

Smith, Jacquelin. Animal Communication. Galde Press, Inc. 2005. ISBN-13: 978-1931942249.

Stein, Diane. Natural Healing for Dogs and Cats. Crossing Press 1993. ISBN-13: 978-0895946140.

HOW TO ORDER DVDS, CDS, & BOOKS

To buy any of the following programs go to
www.healingreiki.com or call 949-263-4676

BOOKS BY STEVE MURRAY

Cancer Guided Imagery Program
For Radiation, Chemotherapy, Surgery,
And Recovery

Reiki The Ultimate Guide
Learn Sacred Symbols and Attunements
Plus Reiki Secrets You Should Know

Reiki The Ultimate Guide Vol. 3
Learn New Reiki Aura
Attunements Heal Mental &
Emotional Issues

Reiki The Ultimate Guide Vol. 4
Past Lives and Soul Retrieval
Remove Psychic Debris and Heal
your life

Animal Psychic Communication
Plus Reiki Pet Healing

Reiki The Ultimate Guide Vol. 2
Learn Reiki Healing with Chakras
plus New Reiki Attunements
for All Levels

Reiki False Beliefs Exposed
For All Misinformation
Kept Secret By a Few Revealed

Reiki The Ultimate Guide Vol. 5
Learn New Psychic Attunements to
Expand Psychic Abilities & Healing

DVDS BY STEVE MURRAY

Reiki Master Attunement
Become A Reiki Master

Reiki 2nd Level Attunement
Learn and Use the Reiki Sacred
Symbols

A Reiki 1st
Aura and Chakra
Attunement Performed

A Reiki Prosperity Attunement

Successfully Preparing for Cancer
Radiation
Guided Imagery and Subliminal
Program

Preparing Mentally & Emotionally
For Cancer Surgery
A Guided Imagery Program

Preparing Mentally & Emotionally
For Cancer Radiation
A Guided Imagery Program

Reiki 1st Level Attunement
Give Healing Energy To Yourself
and Others

Reiki Psychic Attunement
Open and Expand Your Psychic
Abilities

Reiki Healing Attunement
Heal Emotional-Mental-Physical-
Spiritual Issues

Reiki Psychic Attunement Vol. 2
New Attunements to Expand
Psychic Abilities

Preparing Mentally & Emotionally
For Cancer Chemotherapy
A Guided Imagery Program

Preparing Mentally & Emotionally
For Cancer Recovery
A Guided Imagery Program

Pain Relief Subliminal Program
Let Your Unconscious Mind Do It

Destroying Cancer Cells
Guided Imagery and Subliminal Program

30-Day Subliminal Weight Loss
Program Let Your Unconscious
Mind Do The Work!

Cancer Fear and Stress Relief Program

Successfully Preparing for Cancer
Chemotherapy
Guided Imagery and Subliminal
Program

MUSIC CDs BY STEVE MURRAY

Reiki Healing Music
Attunement Volume I

Reiki Healing Music
Attunement Volume II

Reiki Psychic Music
Attunement Volume I

Reiki Psychic Music
Attunement Volume II

Reiki Aura Music Attunement

Reiki Chakra Music Attunement

DVDs BY BODY & MIND PRODUCTIONS

Learning To Read The Tarot
Intuitively

Learning To Read The Symbolism
Of The Tarot

Mind Fitness Workout:
"Program the Mind for Weight
Loss as you Exercise" Dance Workout

How to Contact Spirits, Angels &
Departed Loved Ones:
A step-by-step Guide

Mind Fitness Workout:
"Program the Mind for Weight
Loss as you Exercise" Walking Workout

How to Contact Spirits Vol. 2
Learn to use a Spirit/Ouija Board
and Hold a Séance

Mind Fitness Workout:
"Program the Mind for Weight
Loss as you Exercise" Fitness Workout

Remove Psychic Debris & Heal Vol.1
Access a Past life

Remove Psychic Debris & Heal Vol.2
Soul Retrieval

Remove Psychic Debris & Heal Vol.3
Detach Negative Psychic Cords

More of what people are saying...

I also felt the attunement from Steve's DVDs. They are wonderful, life altering, and being an absolutely blessed experience. Reiki is for everyone willing to learn and he provides it. Thanks for not coloring inside the lines. Namaste. *B.J.*

Empowering!! I am by nature open-minded, but cautious. I read Steve's website top to bottom and was inspired by the truth as I read it. It resonated with something deep inside me. I was very drawn to his openness and perspectives on Reiki and decided that this was the right path to follow. I have not been disappointed at all!! Very congruent in all his writing and his mission statement. *O.W.*

I am glad to have found at last the information I need in Steve's Guides and DVDs. At last I feel my work with Reiki will really take off. I have much to learn, but now I have the resources. My thanks to a courageous and excellent teacher, Reiki Master Steve Murray. *E.B.*

I bought this DVD on the recommendation of a Tarot reader who belongs to a metaphysical discussion group. She called it very prophetic and I have to say . . . this DVD delivers! It gives simple instruction on detaching negativity and explains in good detail how to do this for yourself and others! I recommend this DVD because it is very easy to understand, down to earth, and quite interesting! *C.A.*

I have most of Steve's books and DVDs and they are wonderful. I just received the DVDs in his Remove Psychic Debris and Heal series and this might be his best work yet. I highly recommend them if you feel you or somebody in your life might have Psychic Debris, or if you have an interest in Past Lives, Soul Retrieval, and removing Psychic Cords. *E.S.*

I ordered this book with hopes of understanding Reiki. To my pleasant surprise, this book exceeded that. Included in this book are Reiki history, what Reiki is, how Reiki can be used, Reiki symbols, and how attunements are given (illustrated steps). To top it all off, the book is very easy to understand and instructions for attunements are clear. This is an excellent book to have in your Reiki library. *P.A.*

The Reiki Ultimate Guides and DVDs give you a working knowledge of how to draw the symbols and the process of attunements, both receiving and giving. The pictures are very easy to follow and detail hand positions and how and where to draw the symbols for passing on attunements. *S.M.*

I have recently received these 3 DVDs and was very excited by the explicit step-by-step way that Steve Murray teaches how to remove the Negativity that I couldn't seem to shake. He explains what to do and why. I can overcome these burdens and be more fulfilled and Happy!! Thanks, Steve, you always come through when I need your help. I have found all of the DVDs and books easy to understand. *K.H.*

I am a beginner in the study of Reiki and I was totally thrilled to find this book by Steve Murray. I have read it cover to cover and use it as a ready reference constantly. I was so pleased that I have since purchased his other books on Reiki and a couple of his DVDs. If you are just starting into the Reiki field and are not sure where to begin, I strongly advise Steve's books. You will find everything you need in easy to understand language and photos. *J.B.*

I am working on my master's in mental health counseling. I will be using methods like meditation and Reiki in my practice. Steve Murray has taken Reiki and made it available to everyone at a fair price. His books and tapes work. Bravo Steve! *A.F.*

About the Author

Steve Murray is an Usui Reiki Master and the author of the global best selling Reiki The Ultimate Guide books. Steve also has a series of 25 healing programs on DVD. The DVD subjects include Reiki Attunements; Cancer Guided Imagery; weight loss, pain, fear, and stress relief, just to name a few. And he has produced six Reiki CDs for healing.